Landmark Events in American History

The Scottsboro Case

Michael V. Uschan

WORLD ALMANAC® LIBRARY

#53306232

6-12-08

Please visit our web site at: www.worldalmanaclibrary.com
For a free color catalog describing World Almanac® Library's list of high-quality books and multimedia programs, call 1-800-848-2928 (USA) or 1-800-387-3178 (Canada). World Almanac® Library's fax: (414) 332-3567.

Library of Congress Cataloging-in-Publication Data

Uschan, Michael V., 1948-
    The Scottsboro case / by Michael V. Uschan.
      p. cm. — (Landmark events in American history)
    Includes bibliographical references and index.
    Summary: Discusses the legal case in which nine African American men were falsely accused of rape, the trials and appeals thereafter, and the historical background regarding the lack of civil and legal rights for African Americans.
    ISBN 0-8368-5388-1 (lib. bdg.)
    ISBN 0-8368-5416-0 (softcover)
    1. Scottsboro Trial, Scottsboro, Ala., 1931—Juvenile literature. 2. Trials (Rape)—Alabama—Scottsboro—Juvenile literature. [1. Scottsboro Trial, Scottsboro, Ala., 1931. 2. African Americans—Civil rights—History. 3. Trials (Rape).] I. Title. II. Series.
KF224.S34U82   2004
345.73'02532'0976195—dc22
                  2003061390

First published in 2004 by
World Almanac® Library
330 West Olive Street, Suite 100
Milwaukee, WI 53212 USA

Produced by Discovery Books
Editor: Sabrina Crewe
Designer and page production: Sabine Beaupré
Photo researcher: Sabrina Crewe
Maps and diagrams: Stefan Chabluk
World Almanac® Library editorial direction: Mark J. Sachner
World Almanac® Library art direction: Tammy Gruenewald
World Almanacs Library production: Jessica Morris

Photo credits: AP/Wide World Photos: pp. 5, 18, 20, 21, 23, 29, 35, 37, 40; Chicago Historical Society: p. 28; Corbis: cover, pp. 4, 6, 7, 8, 9, 10, 12, 13, 14, 15, 16, 17, 19, 22, 24, 25, 27, 20, 31, 32, 33, 34, 36, 38, 39, 41, 42, 43; Leroy Gist: p. 16; University of Virginia, Albert and Shirley Small Special Collections Library: p. 26.

Printed in the United States of America

1 2 3 4 5 6 7 8 9 08 07 06 05 04

Contents

Introduction

Arrest and Conviction

On March 25, 1931, nine young men and boys were arrested when they were pulled off a train as it arrived in the small town of Paint Rock, Alabama. Just two weeks later, in nearby Scottsboro, Alabama, all nine of the Scottsboro Boys—as they became known—were convicted of **rape**, and eight of them were sentenced to death.

The Scottsboro Case, however, was not about rape because none had taken place. It was about the **prejudice** that white southerners had toward African Americans. The Scottsboro Boys were put on trial because they were black. In the 1930s, especially in the **South**, whites believed that African Americans were inferior, and this prejudice meant blacks did not get the legal rights they deserved as U.S. citizens.

This photograph of the Scottsboro Boys with their attorney Samuel Leibowitz (seated, front left) was taken in 1933.

Color is Evidence

"The law of the white folks in the South is, 'Don't you dispute my word, nigger.' If a white person says you did something, you did it. Color is more important than **evidence** down there. Color is evidence. Black color convicts you."

Haywood Patterson, one of the Scottsboro Boys, Scottsboro Boy, 1950

Years of Imprisonment

In the years that followed their arrests, the nine youths in the Scottsboro Case fought to prove their innocence. Even after one of the women who had accused them admitted she had been lying, the Scottsboro Boys remained in prison. For years, they lived in fear that they would be executed.

The Scottsboro Case was reported around the nation and the world. The news coverage showed how Alabama's justice system denied the Scottsboro Boys their legal rights for one reason only—their race. The young men became a symbol of the brutality and inequality of life in the southern United States.

The Scottsboro Boys were eventually released, but only after several years. None of them really recovered, and only one, Clarence Norris, went on to live a normal life and gain a full pardon.

The Scottsboro Boys were held in prison for between five and sixteen years. Like other facilities in the South in the 1930s, prisons were **segregated**. This is a prison in Georgia in 1937.

Humiliating Names

In the South, white people used the term "boy" to address a black male, even an adult. The word "boy" was meant to humiliate African-American men by reminding them daily that white people did not respect them. An even more crude racist name often used in the 1930s was "nigger," a degrading form of "Negro." "Negro" or "colored" were more respectful terms, the equivalent of saying "African American," "person of color," or "black" today.

Chapter 1

Segregation and Depression

Abraham Lincoln was president of the United States during the Civil War of 1861–1865, when the South fought the North. During the course of the war, Lincoln became determined to end slavery and issued the Emancipation Proclamation in 1863.

Slavery in the United States

In 1776, the Declaration of Independence declared that "all men are created equal," and that was the principle on which the United States was founded. For nearly a century, however, that promise of equality was denied to the millions of black people who lived as slaves in the South.

In 1863, President Abraham Lincoln issued a declaration to the South. Called the Emancipation Proclamation, it declared that "all persons held as slaves shall be forever free." Although it was an important action, the proclamation did not have much immediate effect, mostly because the Southern slave owners, at war with the United States in the Civil War, defied the proclamation. In 1865, the Thirteenth Amendment to the Constitution eventually freed African Americans from being owned. But it could not liberate them from the **racist** whites, who continued to deny blacks their **civil rights**.

Jim Crow Laws

From 1865 to 1877, after the Civil War, the **federal** government controlled the governments of southern states. In that period, called Reconstruction, federal officials attempted to protect African Americans against white **discrimination**.

When Reconstruction ended, however, southern states began passing laws that denied African Americans such basic rights as being able to vote. The laws replaced slavery with segregation. Blacks could not eat in white restaurants, shop in white stores, attend white schools, or even ride in the same train cars. Some states passed laws making marriage

A movie house in Pensacola, Florida, in the 1930s had a separate entrance at the back for African Americans. Once inside, blacks and whites sat in separate parts of the theater.

Jim Crow

The character Jim Crow originated in the 1830s in a song performed by Daddy Rice, a white entertainer who performed in minstrel shows. Minstrel performers darkened their faces so they would look black, and they performed songs and dances that depicted black people as lazy, stupid, and immoral. White people enjoyed such shows, and the Jim Crow character became well known and popular. During the time of segregation, the term was used to refer to racist laws and actions that deprived blacks of their civil rights. For instance, the few cars on trains that African Americans were allowed to sit in were known as the "Jim Crow" cars.

The NAACP did everything it could to call public attention to the terrible practice of **lynching**. This was when a black person would be tortured and often killed by a group of white people, usually for a small or imagined offense.

between black people and white people a crime. Such laws became known collectively as "Jim Crow" laws, named after a fictional character.

Living Under Segregation

There was little that southern blacks could do about segregation. Southern whites controlled every level of government because African Americans could not vote and therefore could not elect leaders to help them. Whites owned most of the businesses and refused to hire African Americans for anything but low-paying positions, such as laborers, cooks, or maids. There were laws that said where black people could live, work, and go to school. In every way they could, white people in the South made sure African Americans were denied their rights and freedoms.

Speaking Out

Racism existed in the rest of the United States, but people in northern and western areas were somewhat more **integrated** than in the South and used the same public facilities. Some African Americans in northern states were able to receive a good education and get decent jobs. There was more freedom and more opportunity for people to speak out against the inequality suffered by their fellow African Americans in the South. One of the most fiery and outspoken fighters for racial equality was Harvard University graduate W. E. B. Du Bois.

In *The Souls of Black Folk* in 1903, Du Bois wrote that the most serious "problem of the Twentieth Century is the color line," a reference to the racial divide between blacks and whites. Du Bois worked tirelessly to improve the lives of African Americans by forcefully writing and speaking on the subject. In 1909, Du Bois helped found the National Association for the Advancement of Colored People (NAACP), which became the most powerful group working for African-American civil rights.

The Great Depression

Despite the efforts of Du Bois and others, African Americans made little progress against racism, especially in the South. The Great Depression, which began in 1929 and lasted through the 1930s, made things even worse. In that period, a nationwide economic crisis caused extreme poverty and the loss of millions of jobs. Black people had always held the worst jobs—the ones that were hardest, dirtiest, and paid the least, such as washing dishes or digging ditches—because white people didn't want to do them. In the Great Depression, however, white people took any job they could get. When blacks had to compete with whites for jobs, they usually lost because of discrimination, and so the Great Depression made life even tougher for African Americans.

Sharecroppers were people who farmed small plots of land and split the crop with their landlords. Many black sharecroppers lost their homes and source of food during the Great Depression, when white landowners decided to keep the crops for themselves. These sharecroppers were evicted from their homes in 1939.

On the Train

Travelers ride a freight car to Southern California in 1934. People who were homeless and traveled around in this way were known as "hoboes."

Riding the Freight Trains

During the Great Depression, people traveled long distances around the United States to look for work. Because they did not have any money, many of them traveled for free by jumping on freight trains, riding in or on top of the railway cars that carried goods from one city to another.

On March 25, 1931, the nine young men later known as the Scottsboro Boys hopped on a freight train for a free ride that would change their lives forever. On that day, a Southern Railroad freight train left Chattanooga, Tennessee, for Memphis, Tennessee, along a route that dipped south into Alabama. No one knows for sure how many people climbed aboard the train's forty-two cars, but there could have been as many as fifty illegal riders.

A Fight on the Train

Not long after the train passed Lookout Mountain in Alabama, a fight broke out between black and white riders. It started when one man in a group of several whites, walking along the top of the train, stepped on the hand of eighteen-year-old African American Haywood Patterson, who was going to Memphis to look for work. Patterson later said that he and his three companions did not want trouble, but that the others ordered them to get off because, "This is a white man's train."

The claim was nonsense because all the travelers were illegally riding the train. But whites believed they had the right to order African Americans to do almost anything. When the blacks refused to get off, a fight broke out between seven white men and twelve black men. The African Americans won. "We got the best of it," said Patterson, "and threw them off."

Paint Rock

The men that had been thrown off the train walked to the nearest station—at Stevenson, Alabama—and told officials what had happened. Angered that African Americans had beaten up whites, an official telegraphed to Paint Rock, Alabama, 38 miles (61 kilometers) away, so that the sheriff could arrest the blacks there.

When the train pulled into the small Paint Rock railroad station about 2:00 P.M., it was met by a group of seventy-five angry white men, whom Jackson County Deputy Sheriff Charlie Latham had

This map shows the towns where the Scottsboro Boys were arrested, jailed, and then tried over a period of several years.

The Scottsboro Boys

Charles Weems, at twenty years old, was the oldest of the Scottsboro Boys and the youngest were Eugene Williams, thirteen, and Roy Wright, believed to be twelve. Roy's older brother, Andy Wright, and Clarence Norris were nineteen years old; Haywood Patterson and Olen Montgomery were eighteen; and Ozie Powell and Willie Roberson were fifteen. The Wrights, Patterson, and Williams had known each other before they were arrested.

The young men in the Scottsboro Case were typical of southern blacks in the 1930s. They had lived in poverty all their lives and were poorly educated. Eight were illiterate or nearly so—only Olen Montgomery could read and write. Haywood Patterson left school after the third grade, and the only job he had ever had was as a delivery boy. The mother of Charlie Weems died when he was four, and he was the only one of seven siblings to survive childhood. The others had also experienced difficult childhoods. In addition, Olen Montgomery was nearly blind in one eye, while Willie Roberson had trouble walking and had to use a cane.

The Scottsboro Boys (from left to right) were: Clarence Norris, Olen Montgomery, Andy Wright, Willie Roberson, Ozie Powell, Eugene Williams, Charlie Weems, Roy Wright, and Haywood Patterson.

> ### Hang 'Em
>
> "When the train arrived, it was immediately surrounded by a mob. There was nothing but white people with sticks, guns [and] pitchforks. Folks were hollering, 'Let's take them niggers off of there and put them to a tree and hang 'em.' All of us thought for sure we would be lynched right there, with no questions asked."
>
> *Clarence Norris, interviewed by Kwando Mbiassi Kinshasa,*
> The Man from Scottsboro, *1980*

authorized to arrest the blacks. Armed with pistols, shotguns, and other weapons, the group started pulling African Americans out of train cars, eventually arresting nine young men. Many other people riding the train, both black and white, escaped by running away from what looked like an angry mob.

The nine were tied together, loaded on a truck, and driven to nearby Scottsboro. The youths were told they would be charged with assault and attempted murder for attacking the whites. But their legal situation would soon become much more serious.

The Two Women

When the sheriff's group searched the train cars in Paint Rock, they unexpectedly came upon two white women. The pair were originally mistaken for young men because they were wearing overalls and caps. With them was a white man, Orville Gilley, who had been involved in the fight but had been allowed to remain on the train. The two women identified themselves as twenty-one-year-old

Orville Gilley called himself a "hobo poet" and a wandering entertainer. He became a star witness against the Scottsboro Boys in 1933 when he backed up Victoria Price's accusations of rape, although he had said nothing about witnessing the rapes in 1931.

Hooded members of the Ku Klux Klan burn a fiery cross in 1937. The ritual was intended to terrify blacks and assert white superiority.

Victoria Price and seventeen-year-old Ruby Bates. They were going home to Huntsville, Alabama, having failed to find any employment in Tennessee.

There are conflicting accounts about what the girls told law officers and who made the accusation. But finally one woman said, "We've been raped. All those colored boys raped us." The charge caused outrage, not because rape was such a horrible crime, but because white Southerners believed a white woman having sexual relations with a black man was one of the worst things that could happen. They considered this act so terrible because they believed the two races should remain separate.

At Scottsboro Jail

As word spread that the nine African Americans had raped two white women, some five hundred angry white people gathered around the jail in Scottsboro. Many of them were members of the **Ku Klux Klan**. Some carried lengths of rope and screamed that they would kill the blacks.

The mob demanded that Jackson County Sheriff M. L. Wann give them the prisoners so they could hang them. But Wann stood firm, declaring he and his nine deputies would shoot anyone who tried to break into his jail to get them. Wann then called Alabama Governor Benjamin Miller, who sent National Guardsmen to help protect the prisoners.

The Scottsboro Boys were terrified as the crowd surged around the jail all night. They had a good reason to be frightened. In the first half of the twentieth century, whites sometimes lynched African Americans to punish them for suspected crimes and intimidate other blacks. There had been twenty-one known lynchings in the South in 1930, the previous year..

Identified as Rapists

The next day, the youths had a frightening experience of a different kind. They were taken from their cell to stand before the two women, Price and Bates, to be identified. Price pointed at six of them and said they had raped her. Bates was silent, but the law officers claimed that if Price had been raped, then the other woman must also have been assaulted.

The prisoners realized they were going to be charged with rape. Although they declared they had not harmed the women, the law officers said they did not believe them. Norris said later that he realized at that moment he was in serious trouble. "I knew if a white woman accused a black man of rape, he was as good as dead," said Norris.

Give Them All the Law Allows

"When I saw them nab those Negroes, I sure was happy. Mister, I never had a break in my life. Those Negroes have ruined me and Ruby forever. The only thing I ask is that they give them all the law allows."

Victoria Price, quoted in the Chattanooga Daily Times, March 27, 1931

The Scottsboro Boys needed protection from an angry crowd in 1931, and hostility continued throughout the years of their trials. In this photograph, the National Guard protects the Scottsboro Boys on their way to a meeting with their lawyer in 1933.

Chapter 3

The Scottsboro Boys on Trial

The Trials Begin

On April 6, 1931, a carnival atmosphere reigned in the streets around the Jackson County Courthouse in Scottsboro, Alabama. While a brass band played the popular Civil War song "Dixie," about eight thousand angry yet gleeful whites celebrated the start of the trial of the nine Scottsboro Boys. Two hundred National Guardsmen were in the town to keep the peace if the unruly onlookers became violent. In spite of the soldiers' presence, the angry crowd—many screaming "Kill the niggers!"—terrified the young men as they arrived.

Speedy Trials

The trials before Judge A. E. Hawkins began only twelve days after the **defendants** were arrested. This was very unusual because it meant that the lawyers representing the defendants had very little time to prepare for the trial.

Scottsboro is the county seat of Jackson County, Alabama, and the location of the county courthouse, shown here as it is today. In 1931, when the Scottsboro Boys arrived for their trials, the courthouse was surrounded by an angry and violent crowd.

The Scottsboro Boys were represented by Milo C. Moody, a local lawyer, and Stephen Roddy, a Chattanooga attorney hired by a group of African-American ministers. Roddy was drunk most of the time and Moody was described as incompetent.

Clarence Norris and Charlie Weems were tried together first, then Haywood Patterson alone. Next were Olen Montgomery, Ozie Powell, Willie Roberson, Andy Wright and Eugene Williams all together, and finally Roy Wright. Between April 6 and April 9, Judge Hawkins conducted the four trials at a lightning pace.

> ### Victoria Price's Story
> "There were six to me and three to her. One was holding my legs and the other had a knife to my throat while another ravished me. That one sitting behind the defendants' counsel took my overalls off."
>
> *Victoria Price, April 1931*

Victoria Price on the witness stand during the Scottsboro Case. She would tell her story many times over a period of several years.

The Testimony

In her **testimony**, Victoria Price told dramatically how a dozen African Americans threatened her and Bates with guns and knives and raped them. The other three attackers, she said, escaped when the train got to Paint Rock. Both women claimed several of the blacks raped each of them.

Also **testifying** were local doctors R. R. Bridges and Marvin Lynch, who examined the women less than two hours after the

Dr. R. R. Bridges testified in the Scottsboro trials in 1931 and again in 1933, when this picture was taken. Behind Dr. Bridges, Judge James Horton leans forward to hear the testimony. Both Dr. Bridges and Dr. Lynch said they found no evidence of violent assault on the women.

alleged rapes. They both found physical evidence the women had recently had sex. However, they noted that neither had the kind of bruises or other marks on their bodies that they would have had if their claims that they had been roughly treated were true.

The defendants testified they never touched the women. "I had nothing to do with the raping of the girls," said Weems. "I never

Victoria Price (1911—1982) and Ruby Bates (1915—1976)

Ruby Bates and Victoria Price were almost as poor and uneducated as the nine young men that they claimed raped them. Both had recently lost their jobs in a textile mill in Huntsville, Alabama. They lived in a rundown neighborhood with other victims of the Great Depression, both African Americans and whites.

Price was smarter and much more aggressive than Bates, and she dominated the younger woman in their relationship. Although the southern newspapers tried to portray them as respectable white women, neither Price nor Bates had virtuous backgrounds. Price had already been divorced twice, and it is believed both had made money in Huntsville as prostitutes.

Why did Victoria Price lie? It is likely that both the women were persuaded or forced to lie by local law officers. It could be also that Price stuck to her story because she liked the attention and fame. She died in 1982 without ever having apologized for the lies that had ruined so many lives.

saw anything done to the girls." But Norris, Patterson, and Roy Wright tried to save themselves by accusing the others. "They all raped them," said Wright, who later claimed guards beat him to make him testify against the others.

The Jury

The **jury** at each trial comprised only white people, as southern juries always did. In his final words, prosecuting attorney H. G. Bailey appealed to the **jurors**' racism when he said, "Look at their eyes, look at their hair, gentlemen. They look like something just broke out of the zoo. Guilty or not, let's get rid of these niggers."

A general view of the crowded court-room during the Scottsboro Case shows that the benches were packed with white people. The jury, court officials, and lawyers were all white, too—only the defendants were black.

The Sentences

The jurors found all the defendants guilty. Eight out of the nine were sentenced to death—Roy Wright didn't get the death sentence because one of the twelve jurors said Roy was too young, at twelve years old, to be executed. This disagreement caused a **mistrial**, which meant that it had to be done over again. (In fact, Wright was never tried again, but he remained in prison until 1937.)

Many years after the first trial, Patterson remembered the court-room had looked like "one big smiling white face." When each

Willie Roberson (left) was fifteen and Olen Montgomery (right) was eighteen when they were convicted in 1931. Their **convictions** were later overturned, but they were held in prison without further trials until they were in their twenties.

Justice
"That Justice is a blind goddess
Is a thing to which we black are wise.
Her bandage hides two festering sores
That once perhaps were eyes."

Langston Hughes, poet, Scottsboro Limited, *a book of poetry about the Scottsboro Case, 1932*

death sentence was announced, the crowd outside the court responded with loud cheers. They also sang "There'll Be a Hot Time in the Old Town Tonight," a reference to the fact that the defendants would be electrocuted. The Scottsboro Boys were taken to Kilby Prison near Montgomery, Alabama, to be held until July 10, the date Judge Hawkins had set for their executions.

Unfair Verdicts

Many people around the country believed the **verdicts** were unfair and that the death sentences were too harsh. There was no physical evidence, such as bruises or wounds, to prove the assaults took place, and police never found the knives and guns the women had described. The lack of evidence cast doubt on whether the witnesses had told the truth, and people realized the **defense** attorneys had done a poor job.

Benjamin Miller, the governor of Alabama, received many pleas to show the young men mercy. Even a white lawyer from Atlanta, Georgia, called the death sentences "a barbarous penalty."

A Tug of War

Two groups wanted to help the defendants **appeal** the verdicts.

The NAACP's purpose was to fight for African-American rights. The International Labor Defense (ILD) was a group founded by the Communist Party to help working people.

The two groups began competing to win over the Scottsboro Boys and their families. The ILD had more money than the NAACP, and ILD representatives bought candy and cigarettes for prisoners and gave money to family members. The ILD also began holding rallies and marches in various cities to build support for the defendants. The parents of the defendants soon decided that the ILD would be the best group to help the Scottsboro Boys.

Joseph Brodsky

The ILD's chief attorney, Joseph Brodsky, decided to appeal the verdicts before the Alabama **Supreme Court**. None of the defendants could be executed until the appeal was over, so the youths would be spared death for at least a while.

Richard Moore (right), an officer of the ILD, stands with four mothers of the Scottsboro Boys. In the center stands Ruby Bates, who had accused the boys of rape, but later joined forces with the ILD to try and secure their freedom.

Support for the Scottsboro Boys

In 1925, the Communist Party founded the International Labor Defense to provide legal help for workers battling for their rights against big companies. The group, in an effort to recruit blacks to the Communist Party, also assisted African Americans when whites denied them their civil rights. The ILD, however, was not the only group that supported the Scottsboro boys in their fight for justice. The NAACP stayed involved through the years, supporting the defendants and their families. Later, the NAACP helped the boys find jobs as they were released, and it was NAACP lawyers who assisted Clarence Norris in getting a pardon. Having competed for control of the Scottsboro Boys' case, the ILD and NAACP later collaborated, along with the American Civil Liberties Union, and other groups, when they formed the Scottsboro Defense Committee in 1935. This alliance helped to attract more positive public support for the Scottsboro Boys.

Joseph Brodsky, seen here reading papers during the Scottsboro trials, was the ILD's chief lawyer. He promised the Scottsboro Boys a strong defense team and the support of his organization.

In a hearing that began January 21, 1932, Brodsky challenged the convictions on several grounds. He talked about the lack of black jurors and claimed that Roy Wright should have been tried as a **juvenile**. He argued that the trials were conducted too fast and in a racist environment, and he claimed the defense attorneys had been incompetent. On the other side, Alabama **Attorney General** Thomas G. Knight, Jr., whose father was on the Alabama Supreme Court, argued the verdicts were just.

On March 24, 1932, a year after the arrest of the Scottsboro Boys, the Alabama Supreme Court upheld their convictions, except for that of Eugene Williams. He was granted a new trial as a juvenile because he was only thirteen when

arrested. Roy Wright would also be considered a juvenile in any future legal proceedings.

The U.S. Supreme Court

After this defeat in the Alabama Supreme Court, the ILD appealed the decision to the U.S. Supreme Court, claiming the case violated the Constitution because the Scottsboro Boys' lawyers had failed to defend them adequately. On November 7, 1932, in a decision known as *Powell v. Alabama*, the Supreme Court agreed and ordered new trials for the Scottsboro Boys.

The Second Round Begins

Two years had gone by since the Scottsboro Boys' arrest when the second trials began March 27, 1933. The trials took place in

Born Again from Worrying

"Since the Supreme Court have granted we boys a new trial I think it is my rite to express thanks and appreciation to the whole party for their care. I myself feels like I have been born again from the worrying . . . I have had."

Olen Montgomery, note of thanks to the International Labor Defense

Powell v. Alabama

Powell v. Alabama is a historic legal decision because it affirms the right of people to have a fair trial. The U.S. Supreme Court ruled that the Constitution guaranteed citizens the right to a qualified lawyer in any case in which a defendant could be sentenced to death. The decision was based on the Fourteenth Amendment, which declares citizens cannot be tried "without due process of law" and that all citizens must enjoy "equal protection of the laws." The justices said that the trial judge in the Scottsboro Boys' trials had not given the defendants enough time to hire a good lawyer. They concluded, therefore, that the rights of the defendants to a decent legal defense had originally been denied them.

Samuel Leibowitz (left) and Haywood Patterson (center) prepare for trial at the Morgan County Courthouse in Decatur, Alabama, in 1933. On the right is southern lawyer George Chamlee, a champion of free speech in the South and also on the defense team.

Decatur, Alabama, before Judge James Horton. The Scottsboro Boys were now defended by Samuel Leibowitz, one of the nation's finest attorneys. This time, the defendants would be tried individually, and Haywood Patterson was first.

Victoria Price again testified how she had been raped. Even though Leibowitz questioned her cleverly in an attempt to show she was lying, Price was so smart that he was unable to trap her. Price was "a little bit of an actress," Leibowitz told her at one point, to which Price replied, "You're a pretty good actor yourself."

Bates Changes Her Story

On April 6, 1933, Patterson's trial took a surprising turn when the other accuser, Ruby Bates, appeared as a witness for the defense. In January 1932,

Ruby Bates appears on the witness stand in Decatur in April 1933. She shocked the court when she testified that her previous evidence had been false.

Bates had written her boyfriend to say she had not been raped. In court, Bates confirmed this when she declared the defendants had not attacked her. Bates said she was with Price the entire time they were on the train and that Price had not been raped either. Bates also admitted she and Price had sex with two men the night before the alleged rape incident, which explained why doctors had found physical evidence of that when the women were examined.

When Bates was asked why she had lied, she testified: "I said it but Victoria told me to. She said we might have to lay out [serve] a sentence in jail." So Bates lied because she was worried she might

Made to Lie

"Those policemen made me tell a lie that is my statement because I want too clear myself that is all too if you want to believe, ok. If not that is ok. You will be sorry someday if you had to stay in jail with eight Negroes you would tell a lie two. Those Negroes did not touch me or those white boys. I hope you will believe me the law don't. I love you . . . that is why I am telling you of this thing."

Ruby Bates, letter to her boyfriend Earl Streetman, January 5, 1932

SCOTTSBORO LIMITED

By LANGSTON HUGHES
WITH ILLUSTRATIONS BY
PRENTISS TAYLOR

Price 50 cents

Poet Langston Hughes wrote a series of poems about the Scottsboro Case, published in 1932. This is the cover of *Scottsboro Limited*, illustrated by Prentiss Taylor.

have to go to jail—in the 1930s, she could have been jailed for **vagrancy** or for immoral behavior.

Prejudice Decides Again

Once again, the case would not be decided on facts. Just as the verdicts in the first trial had been tainted by prejudice, so was the verdict in Patterson's second trial. This time, the prejudice was not directed only against blacks. In his closing argument, **prosecutor** Wade Wright argued, "Show them, show them that Alabama justice cannot be bought and sold with Jew money from New York." Defense lawyer Leibowitz was Jewish, and many Southerners hated Jews almost as much as they did African Americans. Some Communist Party members were also Jewish, and it was the Communist Party, after all, that was paying to defend the blacks through the ILD.

At 10:00 A.M. on Sunday, April 9, the jurors gave their verdict: "We find the defendant guilty as charged and fix the punishment at death in the electric chair."

At this point, even some southern newspapers began to condemn the Scottsboro Case. The *News Leader* in Richmond, Virginia, declared in April 1933: "The men are being sentenced to death primarily because they are black."

Judge Horton

On April 18, 1933, Judge Horton postponed the trials of the other defendants, claiming local citizens were so angry over the incident that the defendants could not expect to receive "a just and impartial verdict." Then, on June 22, Horton made a ruling that amazed the nation—he overturned Patterson's conviction. He said he believed the jury had returned a verdict contrary to the evidence, and that a new trial would be needed.

Horton's just and brave decision was based on more than just the evidence presented in court. When Dr. Lynch refused to testify in the second trial, Horton talked to him privately. Lynch told the judge he did not believe that the girls had been raped because there were no physical signs indicating they had been assaulted by a group of several men. "Judge, I looked at both the women and told them they were lying, that they knew they had not been raped, and they just laughed at me," Lynch said. Judge Horton asked him to testify about that, but Lynch refused. He said it would ruin his life because other whites would hate him for helping the Scottsboro Boys.

Horton's decision to order a new trial in the Scottsboro Case was courageous because of the racial hatred that existed in the South. The judge became very unpopular with white voters and was soundly defeated for re-election only a year later. Patterson and the other Scottsboro Boys, however, now had a new chance for justice.

Judge James Horton presiding at the trial of Haywood Patterson in April 1933. Throughout the trial, Horton emphasized to the jury that they should rely on facts, not prejudice, but the jury ignored him.

False Testimony

"[Victoria Price's] testimony was contradictory, often evasive [and] is so contradictory to the evidence of the doctors who examined her that it has been impossible for the Court to reconcile their evidence with hers. The proof tends strongly to show that she knowingly testified falsely in many material aspects of the case."

Judge James Horton, June 22, 1933

The Third Trials

Judge James Horton's attempt at justice would have little impact on the case. On November 7, 1933, the third round of trials began in Decatur before Judge William Callahan. Seven of the Scottsboro Boys were due to be tried. As juveniles, Roy Wright and Eugene Williams were not included. The first trial, of Haywood Patterson, featured the same witnesses as the previous ones except for Ruby Bates, who was afraid to return to the South after being threatened by whites for testifying in the second trial.

A Biased Judge

Judge Callahan made no secret of his prejudices and openly sided with the prosecution against defense attorney Samuel Leibowitz. Every time Leibowitz had an objection about trial procedure, the judge ruled against him. In his final argument, the prosecutor, Attorney General Knight, made an appeal to jurors. "If you let this nigger go," he said, "it won't be safe for your mother, wife or sweetheart to walk the streets of the South." When Leibowitz objected to the claim, Judge Callahan overruled the objection.

In December 1933, the *Daily Worker* published this cartoon ridiculing the prejudice of the judge and jury in the Scottsboro Case.

Judge Callahan:—"I Instruct You to Bring in a Verdict in Accordance With the Laws of Alabama!"
Jury:—"We Git You, Judge"   —By Burck

Scottsboro Jury

Judge Callahan

Guilty Again

Not surprisingly, Patterson was again found guilty and sentenced to death. In Clarence Norris's trial that immediately followed, Norris was also convicted and sentenced to death.

House of Pain

"Alabama's Kilby Prison was really a house of pain. At Kilby, we were caged in narrow cells with small windows which prevented us from seeing anything except a few cells directly in front of you. We weren't allowed to leave our ten-by-twelve cells . . . you were always subject to being cursed at or beaten by the guards. They would always call you 'nigger this' and 'nigger that.' I mean they just didn't know any other way how to talk to you."

Clarence Norris, interviewed by Kwando Mbiassi Kinshasa,
The Man from Scottsboro, *1980*

The trials of the other five Scottsboro Boys were postponed at Leibowitz's request, who said he would appeal the first two verdicts. Patterson and Norris were returned to Kilby Prison near Montgomery to await execution. The other five were held in Birmingham, Alabama. Norris could not understand why officials kept trying them. "I wondered how much longer the state of Alabama would spend its money to prosecute nine innocent boys in order to send them to their deaths," Norris wrote years later.

Protests

Many other people also wondered why Alabama kept prosecuting the Scottsboro Boys even though it appeared they were innocent. Supporters, who believed it was wrong that African Americans could not get a fair trial, held protests in many cities. In one large protest in Washington, D.C., several thousand African Americans marched to the gates of the White House to demand that President Franklin D. Roosevelt free the Scottsboro Boys.

For white Southerners, however, the Scottsboro Case was no longer about rape. It was about their belief that they had the right to treat African Americans as inferior and deny them basic civil

Samuel Leibowitz (1893—1978)

Samuel Leibowitz was the son of Romanian immigrants and grew up in New York City. After finishing law school at Cornell University, he became one of the top criminal lawyers in the United States. Before the Scottsboro Case, he had defended seventy-eight people on charges of first-degree murder, and all but one had been found innocent (the trial for that one had resulted in a mistrial because the jury could not decide if the person was guilty or not). It was a remarkable record. Leibowitz worked

During the Scottsboro trials, Leibowitz had two bodyguards, shown here perched on the running boards of the lawyer's car.

hard to defend his clients, and they admired him greatly. "I love him more than life itself," Haywood Patterson once said. But the southern juries and courts felt otherwise, mostly because Leibowitz was Jewish. Although he made successful appeals to the Supreme Court, Leibowitz had to take a back seat in the courtrooms of Alabama. After the Scottsboro Case, Leibowitz went on to other cases and later served as a judge in New York City.

rights. And they resented Leibowitz and anyone else who told them they had to treat black people as equals.

A Second Supreme Court Decision

The U.S. Supreme Court did not agree with the southern standpoint. Leibowitz had appealed to the Supreme Court, saying Alabama had denied Norris and Patterson their constitutional right to a fair trial because African Americans had not even been considered as potential jurors in their trials. On April 1, 1935, the Court overturned the convictions of Norris and Patterson in a decision known as *Norris v. Alabama*. The ruling said excluding African Americans from the jury denied Norris "equal protection of the laws"

Reversing the Judgment

"In the light of the testimony given by the defendant's witnesses, we find it impossible to accept such a sweeping characterization of the lack of qualifications [for jury duty] of Negroes in Morgan County. The judgment must be reversed."

Justice Charles Evans Hughes, Norris v. Alabama, U.S. Supreme Court, April 1, 1935

The protest march to the White House was led by Mrs. Janie Patterson, mother of Haywood Patterson. She was followed by members of civil rights groups, such as the American Civil Liberties Union, and individual citizens who came to Washington, D.C., to support the Scottsboro Boys.

as required by the Constitution's Fourteenth Amendment. The ruling led, yet again, to new trials.

A Fourth Trial

On January 6, 1936, the seven older defendants appeared again before Judge Callahan in Decatur. For the third time, Patterson was the first to be tried, beginning on January 20. Although twelve

The Supreme Court and Civil Rights

Appealing to the Supreme Court is a long, difficult process, but many historic steps have been made there because people were determined to fight for justice. The job of the Supreme Court is to make sure laws and law courts comply with the Constitution and don't deny people their civil rights. In the mid-1900s, U.S. Supreme Court rulings upheld civil rights several times. The rulings in the 1930s on the Scottsboro Case led to more African Americans being included on juries. The Fourteenth Amendment was used again in a very important civil rights case in 1956, during the Montgomery bus boycott, when the Supreme Court ruled that segregation on buses was unconstitutional.

Another important victory concerned a third-grader, Linda Brown, who had been denied access to a neighborhood school because she was black. In 1954, in *Brown v. Board of Education of Topeka*, the Supreme Court overruled its own earlier decision that segregation in education was acceptable if equal facilities were offered. The policy of "separate but equal" in education, the court ruled, was not constitutional.

blacks were among those called for jury duty, none was chosen. But by considering black people for jury duty, the court said, it had conformed to the Supreme Court ruling.

Victoria Price was again the star witness, and Knight once more prosecuted the defendants. This time, Leibowitz was not in charge of the defense. He remained as an advisor but allowed several other lawyers to try the case because southern whites hated him so much that he feared he would hurt his clients.

On January 23, 1936, Patterson was found guilty for the fourth time. This time, however, he was sentenced to seventy-five years in prison instead of death. The reduced sentence was a compromise because one of the jurors thought he was innocent.

A Violent Incident

The next day, on January 24, while the defendants were being driven to the Birmingham jail, Ozie Powell and Morgan County Deputy Sheriff Edgar Blalock began arguing. After Blalock hit him in the face, Powell stabbed Blalock with a knife he had somehow obtained. Sheriff J. Street Sandlin then shot Powell in the head. (Powell survived, but never recovered completely and had reduced mental abilities the rest of his life.) The incident caused a long delay in the other trials.

The Scottsboro Case trials from 1933 to 1937 were held not in Scottsboro but in Decatur, Alabama, in this courthouse. Officials had the case moved there in the hope of quick convictions under Judge Callahan.

It was during the 1937 trial of Ozie Powell, shown here in the Decatur court-room, that five of the nine rape charges were unexpectedly dropped. Ozie Powell was not freed, however, because of his assault on a prison officer the previous year.

The Final Trials

Norris's third trial finally began July 12, 1937. Callahan was again the judge and, as Norris described it, Ruby Bates once more "told her tired old lies." It only took four days for another guilty verdict and death sentence.

The trials of the other Scottsboro Boys continued over two weeks in a courtroom so hot and steamy that one defense attorney collapsed. In their trials, Andy Wright and Charlie Weems were also found guilty, with Wright sentenced to ninety-nine years in prison and Weems to seventy-five years.

Dropped Charges

When Ozie Powell's trial began July 23, however, surprising things began to happen. The rape charges against Powell were dropped, but he was sentenced on July 24 to twenty years in prison for his stabbing of the Morgan County deputy, Edgar Blalock.

As soon as Powell was sentenced, defense and prosecution attorneys, including Leibowitz, met with Judge Callahan. Within a few minutes, Leibowitz turned and walked out of the courtroom and went to the county jail to get Olen Montgomery, Roy Wright, Willie Roberson, and Eugene Williams. He put them into two waiting cars and sped away. Amazingly, the rape charges had been dropped, and the four young men had been freed.

A Surprising Decision

Prosecutor Thomas Lawson explained that the court had now determined Roberson and Montgomery had not raped the women, even though Price still claimed they had. As for Eugene Williams and Roy Wright, they were juveniles at the time of the incidents, and had already served six and a half years in prison. In view of those facts, Lawson said, "the state thinks the end of justice would be met at this time" by releasing them.

The five left in prison were understandably demoralized and angry. As Norris said later, "It was the saddest day of my life."

Two photographs in 1937 tell two different stories: on the right Willie Roberson (far right) and Eugene Williams happily celebrate their freedom. On the left, Haywood Patterson is left behind in Kilby Prison with a seventy-five-year sentence.

35

Southern Justice

Why the Deal Was Made

The compromise in the Scottsboro Case that allowed four defendants to go free confused everyone. If five were not guilty, people thought, then surely none of them was guilty. In an editorial, the *Times-Dispatch* in Richmond, Virginia echoed popular opinion that the outcome of the latest trials was "a virtual clincher that all nine Negroes are innocent." Why, then, did only four go free?

Three thousand people greeted Samuel Leibowitz and the four freed Scottsboro Boys at Penn Station, New York City, on July 26, 1937, after a six-year battle in the Alabama courts. Leibowitz is destroying his straw hat in a victory ritual.

In early 1937, Alabama Attorney General Thomas G. Knight had begun meeting in secret with Samuel Leibowitz. Alabama had grown weary of trying the defendants, partly because of the expense but mainly because news coverage portrayed Alabamans as mean-spirited racists. Even Grover Alexander Hall of the *Montgomery Advertiser*, who had firmly backed all the trials, pleaded in June to "throw this body of death away from Alabama."

A Compromise

All nine had originally been convicted on the same evidence, but Knight worried that dropping the charges against all the boys at once would infuriate Southerners. He was only willing to free the four who appeared the most harmless: the two youngest defendants, Eugene Williams and Roy Wright, along with Olen Montgomery and Willie Roberson, whose physical disabilities had always made them unlikely suspects. The compromise included a promise that the others could be **paroled** as early as 1938.

Freedom at Last

On August 19, 1938, Governor Bibb Graves changed the death sentence for Clarence Norris to life in prison, but he did not parole anyone. And on November 5, 1938, Graves broke the promise and denied parole to the remaining Scottsboro Boys, claiming they were still dangerous. Graves

Fifteen years after his arrest, Clarence Norris walked out of Kilby Prison, paroled at last.

apparently backed away from the deal because he feared freeing the men would ruin his political career. Not even a letter from President Franklin Roosevelt on December 7, 1938, urging that Graves grant the paroles, could sway him.

Four of the five prisoners were eventually paroled after several years. Charlie Weems was freed in 1943, Clarence Norris and Andy Wright in 1944, and Ozie Powell in 1946.

Haywood Patterson was never paroled. But on July 17, 1947, sixteen years after his wrongful arrest, he led several other prisoners in a successful escape from a prison farm near Kilby Prison and made his way to Detroit, Michigan. When Alabama officials discovered where he was and tried to have him returned to prison, Michigan Governor G. Mennen Williams refused to send him back. Three years after his escape, in December 1950, Patterson was

Haywood Patterson remained behind bars, watching as one after another of the Scottsboro Boys was released. He escaped in 1947, only to die in prison five years later.

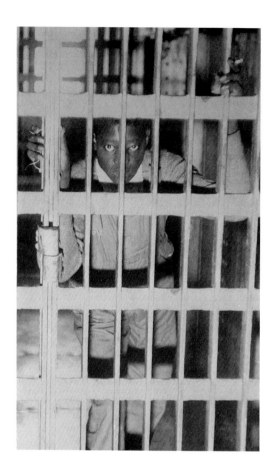

arrested for killing a man in a fight. He died of cancer in prison in August 1952.

The South

Despite the tragic consequences of the Scottsboro Case and the publicity it generated, nothing changed about the way whites mistreated African Americans in the South. White people continued to keep black people segregated and deny many of their rights, including being able to vote and serve on juries. The Ku Klux Klan continued to terrorize African Americans, beating them and sometimes killing them for small or imagined offenses.

The plight of southern blacks would not begin to change significantly until the civil rights movement began to gain strength in the mid-1950s. Until then, thousands of innocent Americans like the Scottsboro Boys would suffer at the hand of white racists.

Escape

"We were thinning rice at that time, working in the rice field. That was about five miles from the main prison. We worked until the sun was almost completely out of sight. We were somewhere on a river bottom. All in there it was high corn. The dog warden had taken off with the hounds. So I got all the boys together and said, "Let's go." We hit for the woods. Captain Nutley, he fired several shots. I didn't run very far down the corn, just out of sight. I told the others, "Get going. Go fast."

Haywood Patterson, describing his prison escape, Scottsboro Boy, *1950*

The Emmett Till Case

An example of southern injustice was the 1955 murder of Emmett Till. The fourteen-year-old from Chicago, Illinois, was visiting relatives in Money, Mississippi. In response to a dare by friends, he whistled at and spoke to Carolyn Bryant, a white woman. It was a harmless action, but on the night of August 28, several men with guns came and took him from the house where he was staying. Three days later, Emmett Till's body was found in the Tallahatchie River, where he had been dumped after being beaten to death.

Mose Wright takes the stand to identify his nephew Emmett Till's white killers, a brave move for a black man in the segregated South. The accused were acquitted anyway.

Ray Bryant, the woman's husband, and J. W. Milam were charged in the slaying. But despite testimony that showed they were guilty, a white jury **acquitted** them. The Scottsboro Case had shown that any black person charged with hurting a white was automatically guilty. The Till trial showed the other side of southern justice—that it was all right for white people to injure or even kill African Americans.

Norris's Pardon

Most of the Scottsboro Boys led troubled lives after their release. They struggled to hold jobs, drank heavily, and got into more trouble. The Scottsboro Case had ruined their lives.

Of the nine defendants, Clarence Norris had the most successful life. He moved to New York City, married, raised a family, and began the process of seeking a full pardon from Alabama. A pardon would mean an official statement would be made that he had never done anything wrong.

On November 29, 1976, in Montgomery, Norris received the pardon from an unlikely source, Alabama Governor George Wallace, who had always tried to deny African Americans their civil rights. The last surviving defendant in the Scottsboro Case, Norris died in a New York City hospital on January 23, 1989, at the age of seventy-six.

Clarence Norris was the only one of the Scottsboro Boys to receive a full pardon. He is shown here at a press conference at the time of his pardon in 1976.

No Hate

"I have no hate toward any creed or color. I like all people, and I think all people accused of things which they didn't commit should be free. I wish these other eight boys were around because their lives were ruined by this thing too."

Clarence Norris, after accepting his pardon, November 29, 1976

A Television Show

By 1976, the Scottsboro Case had faded into obscurity, but that year, the NBC television network broadcast a show called "Judge Horton and the Scottsboro Boys." Victoria Price had married a tobacco farmer in Flintville, Tennessee, and was now known as Katherine Victory Street. When the show was aired, she filed a libel lawsuit because it portrayed her as a prostitute and liar. Street settled out of court with NBC for an undisclosed amount of money that she used to buy a small house, something she said had always been her dream. Ruby Bates also filed a lawsuit, but she died before it was settled.

Nothing But the Truth

"I ain't done nothing but told the truth and nothing but the truth. I told it in every trial . . . there has been over a thousand pages and every one of my pages is alike and if I had to do it all over . . . it would be the same thing again. Truth will stand where a lie will fall."

Katherine Victory Street (Victoria Price), after NBC broadcast the television show "Judge Horton and the Scottsboro Boys," 1976

On July 2, 1964, President Lyndon B. Johnson signs the Civil Rights Act in the presence of civil rights leaders and government officials. Such advances in civil rights came too late for the Scottsboro Boys and other victims of segregation and racism in the South.

Conclusion

The struggle for racial equality moved forward through nonviolent protest in the 1950s and 1960s, under the leadership of Martin Luther King, Jr., (center left in white cap).

After the Scottsboro Case

The color of their skin was enough to convict the Scottsboro Boys of a crime they did not commit. In their case, justice and evidence did not matter as much as the fact that they were black. In the South of 1931, their color meant they must be guilty of anything a white person accused them of.

> **Endless Generations**
> "The victim may die quickly and his suffering cease, but the uniform lessons of all history illustrate, without exception, that its perpetrators not only pay the penalty themselves, but their children throughout endless generations."
>
> *Judge James Horton, June 22, 1933*

The Scottsboro Case, however, did have an important positive impact. It was one of the earliest cases that made people in the United States and other parts of the world aware of the terrible injustice that existed in southern states. Years later, the trial of Emmett Till's murderers and the struggle of African Americans in the Montgomery bus boycott of 1955 and 1956 added to that awareness and prepared the way for the civil rights movement of the 1950s and 1960s.

Race and Justice Today

More than seventy years later, the color of a person's skin still influences the U.S. criminal justice system. African Americans make up only about 12 percent of the nation's population, but there are nearly as many blacks as whites in jails and prisons. Poverty and poor family life are partly to blame, but **racial profiling**, a form of racial discrimination, is also a factor. It appears, for example, that African Americans have been unfairly targeted in the nation's war on drugs. Even though statistics show there are many more white than black drug users, about 62 percent of people in jail on drug charges are African Americans, whereas only 36 percent of them are white.

Thurgood Marshall (top right), was a lawyer at the NAACP during the time of the Scottsboro Case. He became the first African American appointed to the Supreme Court. This photograph of the justices was taken in 1967.

The Legacy of the Scottsboro Case

Despite the worldwide attention the Scottsboro Case received, it did not bring southern blacks any immediate relief from the racism that denied them their basic rights on a daily basis. And sadly, the racism that destroyed the lives of the Scottsboro Boys still affects African Americans today. In fact, the Scottsboro Case and similar cases are still influencing the South. Resentment and bitterness at years of unfair treatment is a cause of the general animosity and distrust that still exists between the races.

Time Line

1909   ■ NAACP is founded.

1929   ■ Great Depression begins.

1931   ■ March 25: Nine youths are arrested in Paint Rock, Alabama.
April 6: Scottsboro Case trials begin before Judge A. E. Hawkins.
April 6–9: Scottsboro Boys are tried, convicted, and sentenced to death;
trial of Roy Wright ends in a mistrial.
June 22: Executions are postponed pending appeal to Alabama
Supreme Court.

1932   ■ January 5: Ruby Bates admits she was not raped in letter to Earl Streetman.
March 24: Appeal to Alabama Supreme Court fails.
November 7: U.S. Supreme Court reverses convictions in *Powell v. Alabama*.

1933   ■ January: ILD retains Samuel S. Leibowitz to defend Scottsboro Boys.
March 27: Second round of trials begin.
April 9: Haywood Patterson is found guilty again and sentenced to death.
April 18: Judge Horton postpones rest of second round of trials.
June 22: Judge Horton overturns Haywood Patterson's conviction.
November 7: Third round of trials begins.
November–December: Haywood Patterson and Clarence Norris are again
convicted and sentenced to death.

1935   ■ April 1: U.S. Supreme Court reverses convictions in Patterson v. Alabama.

1936   ■ January 6: Fourth round of trials begins.
January 23: Haywood Patterson is convicted for the fourth time and
sentenced to seventy-five years in prison.
January 24: Ozie Powell stabs deputy sherriff.

1937   ■ July 12–24: Trials and convictions of Clarence Norris, Andy Wright, Charlie
Weems, and Ozie Powell.
July 24: Roy Wright, Eugene Williams, Olen Montgomery, and Willie
Roberson are released.

1938   ■ November 5: Graves denies parole to Scottsboro Boys remaining in prison.

1943   ■ Charlie Weems is released.

1944   ■ Clarence Norris and Andy Wright are released.

1946   ■ Ozie Powell is released.

1947   ■ Haywood Patterson escapes from prison.

1955   ■ Murder of Emmett Till.

1976   ■ October: Clarence Norris is pardoned by Alabama Governor George Wallace.

Glossary

acquit: pronounce a person not guilty.

alleged: stated but not yet proven.

appeal: ask a higher court to examine a trial verdict and overturn it.

attorney general: chief law officer of a state or nation, who represents the government and citizens in criminal cases.

civil rights: basic rights—such as freedom of movement, ownership of property, voting, education, and choice of religion and political beliefs—of every person.

conviction: act of declaring a person guilty of a crime.

defendant: person charged with a crime.

defense: legal representative who speaks in favor of a defendant.

discrimination: showing of preference for one thing over another. Racial discrimination happens when one racial group is given preference over another racial group.

evidence: something used as proof, especially in a court of law.

federal: having to do with the whole nation rather than separate states.

integrate: mix together people of different races.

juror: person who sits on a jury.

jury: panel of twelve people who decide whether a defendant is guilty or innocent.

juvenile: person who is not yet legally an adult.

Ku Klux Klan: terrorist group in the South that persecuted African Americans.

lynch: to kill by mob action without due process of law.

mistrial: trial that has no legal effect because of an error in how it was conducted.

parole: allow a person to leave prison before serving his or her entire sentence.

prejudice: bias against or dislike of someone because of, for instance, race or religion.

prosecutor: person who takes legal action against someone accused of a crime.

racial profiling: considering a person in a certain way because of his or her race rather than any facts.

racist: having opinions about a person based on race rather than on true qualities.

rape: crime of forcing another person to have sex.

segregate: keep people of different races separate.

South: southern states of Alabama, Arkansas, Florida, Georgia, Louisiana, Mississippi, North Carolina, South Carolina, Tennessee, Texas, and Virginia.

Supreme Court: highest court in the United States or in each state. The U.S. Supreme Court has the power to make final decisions on matters of law and interpretation of the U.S. Constitution.

testify: give evidence at a trial.

testimony: words of a person given in evidence at a trial.

vagrancy: condition of being without a fixed address and regular job.

verdict: decision made by the jury in a trial.

Further Information

Books
Chadwick, Bruce. *Infamous Trials*. Chelsea House, 1997.

Horne, Gerald. *Powell v. Alabama: The Scottsboro Boys and American Justice*. Franklin Watts, 1997.

Kinshasa, Kwando Mbiassi. *The Man from Scottsboro: Clarence Norris and the Infamous 1931 Alabama Rape Trial, in His Own Words*. McFarland, 1997.

Rhym, Darren. *The NAACP* (African American Achievers). Chelsea House, 2001.

Wormser, Richard. *The Rise and Fall of Jim Crow*. St. Martin's Press, 2003.

Web Sites
www.law.umkc.edu/faculty/projects/FTrials/scottsboro University of Missouri web site about the Scottsboro Case covers everything from the legal decisions to the participants to the incident itself.

www.naacp.org The web site of the National Association for the Advancement of Colored People offers historical information and current news about African-American civil rights.

www.pbs.org/wgbh/amex/scottsboro Public Broadcasting System web site based on a television program about the Scottsboro Case includes pictures, official documents, and first-person accounts by the people involved.

Useful Addresses
National Association for the Advancement of Colored People
4805 Mt. Hope Drive
Baltimore, MD 21215
Telephone: (410) 521-4939

Index

Page numbers in *italics* indicate maps and diagrams. Page numbers in **bold** indicate other illustrations.